3
MIRACLE MINDSET

31 Days TO A MIRACLE MINDSET

JOSHUA MILLS

31 DAYS TO A MIRACLE MINDSET
Joshua Mills

Cover by Ken Vail, Prevail Creative, Charlottetown, PEI, Canada.

Interior design by David Sluka

ISBN 978-0-9830789-1-3

Published by New Wine International, Inc.

www.NewWineInternational.org

Printed in the United States of America

Endorsements

Perhaps you, like many others today, eagerly desire to experience the realm of the miraculous in your life. You may have read, heard, or seen others like Joshua Mills as they testify of awesome signs, wonders, and miracles occurring in their lives and ministries. You may have thought, "WOW! I wish I could experience these same miracles in my life."

If this is your desire, then you now have in your hands the most important book after the Bible that you have ever read. You may find yourself reading straight through the entire book as we did initially in one sitting. However, the truths found in this book are skillfully and purposely divided into thirty-one sessions to encourage you to spend a day meditating on and visualizing each of these powerful truths so they can become a reality in your life.

We are blessed to have Joshua Mills as a personal friend. During our many years of relationship, fellowship, and ministering together, we can say that he is a man of integrity. All of the astounding miracles you have heard about in Joshua's life and ministry are true. His ministry is based solidly on the Word of God.

In this powerful, life-changing book, you are about to discover the secret of how you can live in the same realm of glory, experiencing the same or similar signs, wonders, and miracles in your life, as Joshua has for so many years. We challenge you to treasure this book as more valuable than gold or diamonds, and spend time daily for the next month prayerfully meditating and visualizing each of these powerful truths. Look up each of the Miracle Encounters in your Bible and see them becoming a reality in your life. As you do, you will be joining many others on a journey to "31 Days To A Miracle Mindset."

Dr. A.L. & Joyce Gill
Evangelists and Best-selling Authors of *Miracles Are Still Happening* and *God's Promises For Your Every Need*
Gill Ministries, Big Bear Lake, California
www.gillministries.com

REMEMBER THE MIRACLES! This is what has carried me through the most difficult days the Crystal Cathedral ever faced. Remember the miracles! That is what God instructed His children to do. Build a memorial to remember the miracle of the parting of the Red Sea. Entire Psalms are dedicated to remembering the miracles! And this is what Joshua Mills helps us do in *31 Days To A Miracle Mindset*. Remember the miracles that God—the same yesterday, today, and forever—has done, is doing and will do in you and through you!

Dr. Sheila Schuller Coleman, Ed. D.
"The Hour of Power" and Senior Pastor
Crystal Cathedral, Garden Grove, California
www.crystalcathedral.org

In *31 Days To A Miracle Mindset*, Joshua Mills brings a faith building truth, a scriptural basis for that truth, a great quote for the day and a reminder of Biblical accounts of the miraculous. Each page will move you toward a miracle mindset that will, in turn, catapult you into the glory realm of God... where nothing is impossible. This book is a must read for anyone who wants to live in a greater dimension of the supernatural.

Dr. Jeff Walker, D. Min., Psy. D.
Licensed Clinical Psychologist
Senior Pastor, Victory Christian Center
Rancho Mirage, California
www.victorychristian.org

contents

*"A Miracle Is Possible
Wherever Faith Is Unstoppable!"*
–Joshua Mills

FOREWORD BY DR. MIKE MURDOCK

Joshua Mills is making a powerful impact in Christianity.

When he prays, answers come. The response at The Wisdom Center was amazing and people continue to talk about his unique anointing that unlocks such tremendous faith.

31 Days To A Miracle Mindset will benefit thousands around the world.

It is concise.

It is scriptural.

It is believable.

It unleashes…Hope.

It is a perfect gift for anyone…who really needs a miracle from God.

I suggest that you invest in several for friends of yours who are fighting disease, difficulty in their home life, or simply battling Mind-War.

This is a book for…someone in crisis.

It is a book for someone…who wants to see swift and immediate reaction from God to their problems.

Joshua Mills is truly a gift from the Holy Spirit to the Body of Christ. I highly commend his life, his ministry, and his writings. He understands the Authority, Anointing, and Diversity.

Dr. Mike Murdock
Founder, The Wisdom Center
Denton, Texas
www.thewisdomcenter.tv

Receiving a Miracle Mindset

For as he thinks in his heart, so is he.

—Proverbs 23:7 (NKJV)

Over the past few years the Lord has been teaching us a lot about mindsets. The Lord can only move as far as your mind will allow, because everything with God is connected to the element of faith. We must believe! The Bible says that miraculous signs and wonders will fill the lives of believers (Mark 16:17). The Bible also teaches that nothing in life will be impossible for a believer (Matthew 17:20) and that without faith it's impossible to even begin to please

God (Hebrews 11:6). The underlining truth in all of these Scriptures is the fact that we must BELIEVE! Even Jesus Himself could not perform many miracles or heal the sick in His hometown (and He is God!) because of a lack of faith in the hearts of the people.

> *Jesus said to them, "Only in his home-town and in his own house is a prophet without honor." And he did not do many miracles there because of their lack of faith.* —Matthew 13:57-58

Jesus carried the miracle realm with Him everywhere He went. We can read many testimonies of Him performing amazing signs and wonders, healing the sick, cleansing the lepers, raising people from the dead, and yet He couldn't do many miracles in His hometown because these people did not have a miracle mindset. The Bible says that if we don't believe in the miraculous, we won't be able to experience the power of God.

That man should not think he will receive anything from the Lord; he is a double-minded man, unstable in all he does. —James 1:7-8

How do we believe for the impossible? How can we believe for miracles in such troublesome times and through difficult situations? I want to give you three simple keys to receiving a miracle mindset. Begin to use these keys as you go through this powerful study over the next 31 days. Take time to reflect and respond to the revelation using these practical keys:

1. Renew Your Mind With The Word Of God.

Something begins to happen as you meditate upon the Scriptures. As you read and study the Bible, God's supernatural Word will become a catalyst for His supernatural power to become manifest in your life. Suddenly it becomes like water that washes away old mindsets, negative thinking, stubborn habits, and it will even begin to change your vocabulary! *"Do not conform any longer to the pattern of this world, but be transformed by the renewing of your mind. Then you will be able to test and approve what God's will is—his good, pleasing and perfect will"* (Romans 12:2).

2. Focus On The Possibilities Instead Of The Impossibilities.

This will take some practice, but remember the old saying, "Practice makes perfect." Instead of seeing situations and circumstances from a negative perspective, begin realizing that God's plan for your life is greater than any attack of the enemy. Try to stay focused on the things of God. *"Whatever is true, whatever is noble, whatever is right, whatever is pure, whatever is lovely, whatever is admirable—if anything is excellent or praiseworthy—think about such things"* (Philippians 4:8).

3. Recognize That You've Been Given A Promise.

Not only does God want you to focus on His possibilities, He has provided a promise to give you a brand new mind that is filled with His possibilities. It is the mind of Christ (1 Corinthians 2:16). Begin receiving this miracle mindset today! *"Let this mind be in you, which was also in Christ Jesus"* (Philippians 2:5).

Receive A Miracle Mindset

For the next 31 days I am going to give you some powerful thoughts to focus on. These are personal truths that God has spoken to my spirit as I've asked Him to direct my understanding. They are all scripturally based and contain revelation about the miracle realm that will change your life forever!

When you focus on the things of heaven, suddenly the things of heaven begin to focus on you! I believe that at the end of this 31-day journey, your mind will be renewed and you will be living with a "miracle mindset" that will be able to believe God for the impossible!

Remember, *"Faith comes from hearing the message, and the message is heard through the word of Christ"* (Romans 10:17). As you go through these revelations begin looking for the miracles. I believe God is going to demonstrate Himself in new and unusual ways for you.

Many times we miss the miracles because our eyes are not open to see them! Become attentive, alert, and aware of what begins to happen around you over these next days. You are going to be in awe as you journey **31 Days To A Miracle Mindset!**

Enjoy the ride!

9 Important Facts About Miracles

1. Miracles Happen For Those Who Believe!

You must believe that God wants to do it, and that you're qualified to receive it! Every true Believer is a Miracle Receiver! Your believing always affects your receiving. *"But as many as received Him, to them He gave the right to become children of God, even to those who believe in His name"* (John 1:12 NASB).

2. Love Is A Miracle Magnet.

Love is the answer…it always has been and always will continue to be the key ingredient to receiving and administrating God's miracle-working power. The compassion of Jesus Christ towards the sick and hurting released the ability to meet their needs in a miraculous way. *"Jesus had compassion on them and touched their eyes. Immediately they received their sight and followed him"* (Matthew 20:34).

3. Miracles Come To Those Who Seek!

Miracles do not come to the self-righteous, but they are always obtained by the hungry. Whatever you seek you will find! Always remember that you can pursue any miracle from God, but ultimately God chooses the method by which the miracle is received. Do not put limits on how God may bring a miracle into your life. He is unlimited in potential. Discovering God's Word uncovers His miracles. A hungry heart will seek for supernatural solutions from a supernatural source. *"Ask and it will be given to you; seek and you will find; knock and the door will be opened to you"* (Matthew 7:7).

4. Miracles Are Birthed By Faith.

God doesn't respond to the needy, but He always responds to the faith-filled. Do not fear the turmoil of today, or the situations that you are currently facing in your life. They are all subject to change! Your circumstances are not permanent! Fear brings resistance to the future that your faith is able to create. Do not fear but become full of faith! Faith is the catalyst for change and moving in the right direction! *"For we also have had the gospel preached to us, just as they did; but the message they heard was of no value to them, because those who heard did not combine it with faith"* (Hebrews 4:2).

5. Miracles Are Connected To A Sound.

A sound always precedes a miracle. King Jehoshaphat understood this powerful principle and put it into practice, causing his armies to supernaturally win the battle (2 Chronicles 20:12-24). At the dedication of Solomon's temple, the praise went first and the miracle cloud followed (2 Chronicles 5:13). In Acts 16, Paul and Silas released a sound of praise that filled the entire prison and made it shake (this was the original jail-house rock!). After the sound like a mighty rushing wind resounded through the Upper Room, all the people were ignited with a miracle flame of revival. *"The tongue has the power of life…"* (Proverbs 18:21).

Faith-filled words will connect you to a supernatural dimension of blessing because miracles are always connected to a sound… the sound of the gospel…the sound of your testimony…the sound of praise…the sound of your daily declarations and confessions. Praising past your current condition will cause you to receive a miracle transition! *"Suddenly a sound like the blowing of a violent wind came from heaven and filled the whole house where they were sitting. They saw what seemed to be tongues of fire that separated and came to rest on each of them. All of them were filled with the Holy Spirit and began to speak in other tongues as the Spirit enabled them"* (Acts 2:2-4).

6. Fervent Prayer Births Miracles.

Prayer re-focuses your perspective. When you seek the Lord to hear His voice, He will always give you a revelation of victory. Trials that are bathed in prayer become triumphs, and set-backs that are covered in prayer become set-ups! *"And the prayer offered in faith will make the sick person well; the Lord will raise him up. If he has sinned, he will be forgiven"* (James 5:15).

7. Ministering Angels Accelerate Miracle Requests.

When you begin to put your Angels to work, you'll notice an increase in miracle activity in your life. God uses the Angelic realm to release healings, financial breakthroughs, restoration of relationships, and other supernatural phenomenon as directed by the Lord. (I encourage you to obtain a copy of my teaching CD "Ministering With Angels." It will teach you how to activate their assistance in your life – Item #CD-12). *"Do you think I cannot call on my Father, and he will at once put at my disposal more than twelve legions of angels?"* (Matthew 26:53).

8. The Atmosphere You Create Determines The Miracle You Receive.

What type of atmosphere is conducive to producing the miracles you want in your life? I have discovered that playing instrumental piano music in my office causes me and my employees to become more alert, productive, and at peace. Using a simple notepad to schedule my day with a "to-do" list has also helped me in creating an atmosphere of productivity. Whenever I read my Bible and focus on the miracles of Jesus, I find that I am filled with boldness in my spirit to see some of these same miracles take place in my own life. This also happens when I am able to watch DVDs or listen to CDs from other ministers who have great healing and miracle ministries. There is an impartation that comes in that atmosphere. Words, sound, colors, spiritual environment, fragrance, attitude, and relationships all create an atmosphere.

Determine what miracles you want to receive and begin to create an atmosphere that will produce those results. (For further teaching on creating an atmosphere for miracles and success, purchase a copy of my book *Atmosphere* – Item #BK-17.) *"What goes into a man's mouth does not make him 'unclean,' but what comes out of his mouth, that is what makes him 'unclean'"* (Matthew 15:11).

9. Uncommon Boldness Releases Uncommon Miracles.

In order to witness the miracles of God, we must boldly press in to receive them. In Acts 4, the early believers prayed this prayer, "Enable your servants to speak your word with great boldness," because they desired to see the evidence of the gospel released with signs, wonders, and miracles. They understood bold faith always produces bold evidence.

Every miracle is within your reach, but you need to stretch boldly in order to receive it! *"From the days of John the Baptist until now, the kingdom of heaven has been forcefully advancing, and forceful men lay hold of it"* (Matthew 11:12).

31 DAYS TO A

MIRACLE MINDSET

God will always ask you to do something possible so that He can do something impossible!

LUKE 6:38—Give, and it will be given to you. A good measure, pressed down, shaken together and running over, will be poured into your lap. For with the measure you use, it will be measured to you.

HEBREWS 11:6—And without faith it is impossible to please God, because anyone who comes to him must believe that he exists and that he rewards those who earnestly seek him.

MIRACLE ENCOUNTERS

- Widow of Zarephath's meal and oil increased – 1 Kings 17:14-16
- The catch of fish – John 21:6

Day 2

If you believe that miracles happen, they will. If you don't believe that miracles happen, they won't! Become a true believer and you will become a miracle receiver!

MATTHEW 17:20—[Jesus] replied, "Because you have so little faith. I tell you the truth, if you have faith as small as a mustard seed, you can say to this mountain, 'Move from here to there' and it will move. Nothing will be impossible for you."

1 CORINTHIANS 2:5—So that your faith might not rest on men's wisdom, but on God's power.

MIRACLE ENCOUNTERS

- Pillar of cloud and fire – Exodus 13:21-22
- Water into wine – John 2:1-11

Day 3

Your miracle will come by expectation and participation!

ROMANS 12:12—Be joyful in hope, patient in affliction, faithful in prayer.

JAMES 2:17—In the same way, faith by itself, if it is not accompanied by action, is dead.

It is not the objective proof of God's existence that we want but the experience of God's presence. That is the miracle we are really after, and that is also, I think, the miracle that we really get. —Frederick Buechner

MIRACLE ENCOUNTERS

- Aaron's rod blossomed – Numbers 17:1
- Jesus performing many miracles
  – Matthew 14:34-36; Mark 6:45-52

*Fear never produces the
miraculous, but faith always does!
Be faith-filled instead of being
fear-full!*

PSALM 27:1—The LORD is my light and my salvation—whom shall I fear? The LORD is the stronghold of my life—of whom shall I be afraid?

2 TIMOTHY 1:7—For God did not give us a spirit of timidity, but a spirit of power, of love and of self-discipline.

It is impossible on reasonable grounds
to disbelieve miracles.—Blaise Pascal

MIRACLE ENCOUNTERS

- Manna from heaven – Exodus 16:14-35
- Calming the storm – Matthew 8:24-27;
  Mark 4:37-41

In order to be upgraded to first class, you must be willing to let go of your economy.

JUDGES 18:10—When you get there, you will find an unsuspecting people and a spacious land that God has put into your hands, a land that lacks nothing whatever.

PSALM 35:27—May those who delight in my vindication shout for joy and gladness; may they always say, "The LORD be exalted, who delights in the well-being of his servant."

MIRACLE ENCOUNTERS

- **Marah's waters sweetened**
  – Exodus 15:23-25
- **Feeding the four thousand**
  – Matthew 15:32-38; Mark 8:1-9

Day 6

A new revelation from God will always lead you into a new elevation in God.

PROVERBS 18:15—The heart of the discerning acquires knowledge; the ears of the wise seek it out.

EPHESIANS 1:17—I keep asking that the God of our Lord Jesus Christ, the glorious Father, may give you the Spirit of wisdom and revelation, so that you may know him better.

> Miracles are not contrary to nature, but only contrary to what we know about nature.
> —Saint Augustine

MIRACLE ENCOUNTERS

- Bronze serpent healing the Israelites
  – Numbers 21:8-9
- Healing in the temple – Matthew 21:14

Day 7

*Your decisions determine your
destiny. Decide to do the will of
God and you will never fail!*

JOHN 6:40—[Jesus said] "For my Father's will is
that everyone who looks to the Son and believes
in him shall have eternal life, and I will raise him
up at the last day."

1 PETER 2:15—For it is God's will that by doing
good you should silence the ignorant talk of foolish men.

Out of difficulties grow miracles.
—Jean de La Bruyère

MIRACLE ENCOUNTERS

- Walls of Jericho fall down — Joshua 6:6-20
- Healing the ten lepers — Luke 17:11-19

Day 8

God is omnipotent, omnipresent, and omniscient; therefore, He is not limited by time nor is He limited by your limited thinking and preconceived ideas. Open up to the glory realm and He will take you places where you have never been before!

ROMANS 8:28—And we know that in all things God works for the good of those who love him, who have been called according to his purpose.

EPHESIANS 1:11—In him we were also chosen, having been predestined according to the plan of him who works out everything in conformity with the purpose of his will.

MIRACLE ENCOUNTERS

- Aaron's rod blossomed – Numbers 17:1
- Jesus performing many miracles
  – Matthew 14:34-36; Mark 6:45-52

Every divine supernatural miracle begins in the heart of God. He transfers it Spirit to spirit and let's you speak it, so you can see it!

AMOS 3:7—Surely the Sovereign LORD does nothing without revealing his plan to his servants the prophets.

JOHN 15:15—I no longer call you servants, because a servant does not know his master's business. Instead, I have called you friends, for everything that I learned from my Father I have made known to you.

MIRACLE ENCOUNTERS

- Sun and moon stand still
  — Joshua 10:12-14
- Calming the storm — Matthew 8:24-27;
  Mark 4:37-41; Luke 8:23-25

Day 10

Your acceleration is determined by your illumination.
Let there be light!

DEUTERONOMY 29:29—The secret things belong to the LORD our God, but the things revealed belong to us and to our children forever, that we may follow all the words of this law.

JOB 22:28—What you decide on will be done, and light will shine on your ways.

> Faith is to believe what you do not see; the reward of this faith is to see what you believe. —Saint Augustine

MIRACLE ENCOUNTERS

- Creation of the world – Genesis 1:1-31
- Saul's dramatic encounter and conversion – Acts 9:1-19

Day 11

The atmosphere that you create always determines the miracle realm that God can create through you.

ISAIAH 3:10—Tell the righteous it will be well with them, for they will enjoy the fruit of their deeds.

MATTHEW 12:37—[Jesus said] "For by your words you will be acquitted, and by your words you will be condemned."

MIRACLE ENCOUNTERS

- Abraham pleads for Sodom
  – Genesis 18:16-33
- The Believers prayer shakes the place with power – Acts 4:23-31

Day 12

*We don't praise God because of
what we're going through – we
praise God because we know
where we're going to!*

PSALM 89:15-18—Blessed are those who have learned to acclaim you, who walk in the light of your presence, O LORD. They rejoice in your name all day long; they exult in your righteousness. For you are their glory and strength, and by your favor you exalt our horn. Indeed, our shield belongs to the LORD, our king to the Holy One of Israel.

MIRACLE ENCOUNTERS

- Three men delivered from the furnace
  – Daniel 3:19-27
- Paul and Silas miraculously released from
  prison – Acts 16:25-26

Day 13

Your sound contains the power of life and death. What is your sound? What do others hear? Is it positive or negative? Let them hear the sound of glory on your voice – sounds full of life and overcoming victory!

PROVERBS 18:21—The tongue has the power of life and death, and those who love it will eat its fruit.

PROVERBS 12:13—An evil man is trapped by his sinful talk.

MIRACLE ENCOUNTERS

- Jehoshaphat defeats the armies with praise – 2 Chronicles 20:1-29
- Prayer releases the Holy Spirit in the Upper Room – Acts 2:1-4

Day 14

Miracles do not always happen in the place where they are needed, but they always appear in the places where they are seeded. The Word of God is your miracle seed. Plant it in your heart and watch it grow!

2 CORINTHIANS 9:6—Remember this: Whoever sows sparingly will also reap sparingly, and whoever sows generously will also reap generously.

GALATIANS 6:7—Do not be deceived: God cannot be mocked. A man reaps what he sows.

MIRACLE ENCOUNTERS

- A prophetic dream and God's provision
  – Genesis 41:1-56
- Feeding the five thousand
  – Matthew 14:15-21; Luke 9:12-17

42

Day 15

*Being thankful today opens up
doors to be thankful tomorrow!*

PSALM 100:4—Enter his gates with thanksgiving and his courts with praise; give thanks to him and praise his name.

1 THESSALONIANS 5:18—Give thanks in all circumstances, for this is God's will for you in Christ Jesus.

Have an attitude of gratitude! That attitude will flavor everything you do. —Joan Hunter

MIRACLE ENCOUNTERS

- Abraham's ultimate sacrifice and miracle
  – Genesis 22:1-14
- Jesus feeds the five thousand
  – John 6:1-14

Seed the heavens with your praise and rejoice as you experience the showers of blessing that rain down from the cloud of glory!

ZECHARIAH 8:12—[The LORD Almighty says] The seed will grow well, the vine will yield its fruit, the ground will produce its crops, and the heavens will drop their dew. I will give all these things as an inheritance to the remnant of this people.

PSALM 72:6—He will be like rain falling on a mown field, like showers watering the earth.

MIRACLE ENCOUNTERS

- Daniel saved in the lion's den
  – Daniel 6:10-23
- Miraculous signs were done by the Apostles – Acts 2:42-43

Day 17

You are blessed to be a blessing, and that is what causes the miracles in your life to flow over and over again.

GENESIS 12:1-2—The LORD had said to Abram, "Leave your country, your people and your father's household and go to the land I will show you. I will make you into a great nation and I will bless you; I will make your name great, and you will be a blessing."

> I have learned to use the word "impossible" with the greatest caution.
> —Wernher Von Braun

MIRACLE ENCOUNTERS

- Samson kills a lion by supernatural strength – Judges 14:5-6
- Jesus healed the blind man and the mute man – Matthew 9:27-34

Day 18

*Every problem is an invitation
to witness another miracle!*

JEREMIAH 32:17—Ah, Sovereign LORD, you have made the heavens and the earth by your great power and outstretched arm. Nothing is too hard for you.

LUKE 1:37—For nothing is impossible with God.

> You face your greatest opposition when you're closest to your biggest miracle.
> —T.D. Jakes

MIRACLE ENCOUNTERS

- Water from the rock at Rephidim
  — Exodus 17:5-7
- The disciples released from prison
  — Acts 5:17-20

Day 19

*Never change your theology
to fit your situation. God's
Word is eternal while your
problems are temporary!*

ISAIAH 14:24—The LORD Almighty has sworn, "Surely, as I have planned, so it will be, and as I have purposed, so it will stand."

ISAIAH 55:9—"As the heavens are higher than the earth, so are my ways higher than your ways and my thoughts than your thoughts."

I would rather err on the side of faith than on the side of doubt. —Robert Schuller

MIRACLE ENCOUNTERS

- The earth opened up
  — Numbers 16:31-35
- Jesus performed many miracles
  — Matthew 15:29-31

*Deliverance comes with ease when
you touch the glory realm.
Suddenly, you let go of your
struggles and take hold
of your solution.*

PSALM 68:20—Our God is a God who saves; from the Sovereign LORD comes escape from death.

COLOSSIANS 1:13—For he has rescued us from the dominion of darkness and brought us into the kingdom of the Son he loves.

The miracles of earth are the laws of heaven.
—Jean Paul Richter

MIRACLE ENCOUNTERS

- Fire from the Lord — Numbers 11:1-3
- Healing the demoniac — Mark 1:23-28; Luke 4:33-37

Day 21

Salvation requires participation.
God saves us from our own
destruction as soon as we
let go and let God.

PSALM 119:67—Before I was afflicted I went astray, but now I obey your word.

EPHESIANS 2:8—For it is by grace you have been saved, through faith—and this not from yourselves, it is the gift of God.

> Miracles are a retelling in small letters of the very same story which is written across the whole world in letters too large for some of us to see. —C.S. Lewis

MIRACLE ENCOUNTERS

- River Jordan divided – 2 Kings 2:7-8
- Healing the man at the pool – John 5:2-9

Day 22

When you've come to the end of yourself, you've come to the fullness of God.

DEUTERONOMY 4:29—But if from there you seek the LORD your God, you will find him if you look for him with all your heart and with all your soul.

EPHESIANS 3:16-19—I pray that out of his glorious riches he may strengthen you with power through his Spirit in your inner being, so that Christ may dwell in your hearts through faith. And I pray that you, being rooted and established in love, may have power...to grasp how wide and long and high and deep is the love of Christ...that you may be filled to...all the fullness of God.

MIRACLE ENCOUNTERS

- The widow's oil multiplied – 2 Kings 4:2-7
- Jesus healed the crowd near Galilee – Matthew 12:15; Mark 3:7-12

Day 23

*God is love. Perfect love casts out all
fear. Fear not for love is with you.*

ROMANS 12:9—Love must be sincere. Hate what
is evil; cling to what is good.

1 TIMOTHY 1:5—The goal of this command is
love, which comes from a pure heart and a good
conscience and a sincere faith.

Men can see the greatest miracles and miss
the glory of God. What generation was ever
favored with miracles as Jesus' generation?
Yet that generation crucified the Son of God!
We must be careful to see God's glory as
His miracles are released. —Unknown

MIRACLE ENCOUNTERS

- Elijah fed by ravens – 1 Kings 17:1-6
- Raising the widow's son – Luke 7:12-16

When you stop growing you start dying. Let God stretch you today and cause you to reach new levels of victory you've never known before!

PSALM 84:7—They go from strength to strength, till each appears before God in Zion.

2 CORINTHIANS 3:18—And we, who with unveiled faces all reflect the Lord's glory, are being transformed into his likeness with ever-increasing glory, which comes from the Lord, who is the Spirit.

MIRACLE ENCOUNTERS

- Elijah carried up into heaven
  – 2 Kings 2:11
- Raising Lazarus from the dead
  – John 11:1-46

Day 25

*Jesus Christ is big enough inside of
you to solve any difficulty
you may have.*

MATTHEW 13:11—[Jesus] replied, "The knowledge of the secrets of the kingdom of heaven has been given to you, but not to them."

COLOSSIANS 1:26-27—the mystery that has been kept hidden for ages and generations, but is now disclosed to the saints. To them God has chosen to make known among the Gentiles the glorious riches of this mystery, which is Christ in you, the hope of glory.

MIRACLE ENCOUNTERS

- Sound in the mulberry trees
  – 2 Samuel 5:23-25
- Money in the fish's mouth
  – Matthew 17:27

*God will close good doors in order
to lead you through great doors!
Jesus Christ is your open door to
prosperity, healing and victory!
What other door do you need?
He is All in All.*

JOHN 10:9—I am the gate; whoever enters through me will be saved. He will come in and go out, and find pasture.

REVELATION 3:8—I know your deeds. See, I have placed before you an open door that no one can shut. I know that you have little strength, yet you have kept my word and have not denied my name.

MIRACLE ENCOUNTERS

- Jonah in the whale's belly – Jonah 2:1-10
- Jesus walked through the wall
  – Luke 24:36-37; John 20:19-21, 26

Urgently Wanted

OLD POCKET AND WRIST WATCHES WANTED

IN ANY CONDITION

All watches and clocks have some value, working or not.

If you have one tucked away in a drawer, cupboard or box, let me make you an offer, regardless of condition. Below is a list of some of the clocks I urgently require:

MARBLE - BRASS - WALL CLOCKS - INLAID WOOD AND CHIMERS

OLD POCKET & RAILWAY WATCHES - DRESS & FOB WATCHES

ALSO WANTED

MEDALS - SWORDS - BAYONETS - KNIVES - BUCKLES - UNIFORMS - TELESCOPES,

HELMETS AND COMPASSES.

ALSO WANTED

OLD POSTCARD & PHOTO ALBUMS - OLD SILVER ITEMS - PHOTO FRAMES - CUTLERY - TROPHIES

TRINKET BOXES - WRITING BOXES AND OLD LEATHER SUITCASES.

Thank you for your time and patience.

Mr D Mechen

Day 27

*God does not want you
to maintain... He has
called you to succeed!*

JEREMIAH 29:11—"For I know the plans I have for you," declares the LORD, "plans to prosper you and not to harm you, plans to give you hope and a future."

PSALM 40:5—Many, O LORD my God, are the wonders you have done. The things you planned for us no one can recount to you; were I to speak and tell of them, they would be too many to declare.

MIRACLE ENCOUNTERS

- Hundred men fed with twenty loaves
  — 2 Kings 4:42-44
- Healing a woman's infirmity
  — Luke 13:10-17

Day 28

There are no limitations in the Spirit of God. There is no limit to what we can achieve when we walk in the Spirit of Glory.

JOHN 3:17—For God did not send his Son into the world to condemn the world, but to save the world through him.

JOHN 3:34—For the one whom God has sent speaks the words of God, for God gives the Spirit without limit.

Where hope grows, miracles blossom.
— Elna Rae

MIRACLE ENCOUNTERS

- The iron axe-head floats – 2 Kings 6:5-7
- Mass healings and miracles
  – Acts 5:12-16

Day 29

God doesn't promise us that life will be easy, but He does promise us that we will walk in victory! No matter the situation, you are an overcomer through Christ Jesus!

1 JOHN 4:4—You, dear children, are from God and have overcome them, because the one who is in you is greater than the one who is in the world.

ROMANS 4:20-21—Yet he did not waver through unbelief regarding the promise of God, but was strengthened in his faith and gave glory to God, being fully persuaded that God had power to do what he had promised.

MIRACLE ENCOUNTERS

- Thunder destroys the Philistines
  – 1 Samuel 7:10-12
- Paul not harmed by poisonous snake
  – Acts 28:3-6

Day 30

When God's favor rests on your life, it causes you to succeed no matter what the natural circumstance predicts. We are not moved by predictions because we have a prophetic promise of His presence.

PSALM 69:13—But I pray to you, O LORD, in the time of your favor; in your great love, O God, answer me with your sure salvation.

2 CORINTHIANS 6:2—For he says, "In the time of my favor I heard you, and in the day of salvation I helped you." I tell you, now is the time of God's favor, now is the day of salvation.

MIRACLE ENCOUNTERS

- The deadly stew was cured
  — 2 Kings 4:38-41
- Jesus healed the man with dropsy
  — Luke 14:1-6

There are no secrets in the secret place. If you need revelation about something, draw near to God and He will guide you into His heart. Miracles happen in the secret place!

2 KINGS 4:33—He went in, shut the door on the two of them and prayed to the LORD.

MATTHEW 6:6—But when you pray, go into your room, close the door and pray to your Father, who is unseen. Then your Father, who sees what is done in secret, will reward you.

MIRACLE ENCOUNTERS

- Shunammite's son raised from the dead
  — 2 Kings 4:32-37
- Peter raised the woman from the dead
  — Acts 9:40-41

Prayer to Receive Salvation

The Bible says:

That if you confess with your mouth, "Jesus is Lord," and believe in your heart that God raised him from the dead, you will be saved. For it is with your heart that you believe and are justified, and it is with your mouth that you confess and are saved.
—Romans 10:9-10

If you want to give your life to Christ, pray this with me right now:

"Father, thank you for forgiving my sins. Jesus, come into my heart. Make me the kind of person You want me to be. Thank You for saving me. Amen."

The Bible is very clear that *"everyone who calls on the name of the Lord will be saved"* (Romans 10:13). Welcome to the family of God! Please use the contact information at the back of this book to let us know that you have chosen to follow Christ. We also can help you grow strong in your new relationship with Christ.

Albert Einstein said, "There are two ways to live: you can live as if nothing is a miracle; you can live as if everything is a miracle." Determine to live each day as if everything is a miracle. Your natural birth was a miracle, and today your spiritual birth into God's kingdom is another miracle.

Remember that with Jesus, nothing is impossible. So go for it!

Dear Friend,

I believe that you are a kingdom connection! God wants to use you to make a difference in the lives of thousands around the world. Do you believe that?

I would like to invite you to become a *Miracle Worker* with me, and help me take this supernatural message of Jesus Christ and His glory to the far corners of the earth.

Partnership is not simply giving of your finances; it is more. When you become a *Miracle Worker* with this ministry, you will become an integral member of the New Wine International outreach ministry team with special opportunities and privileges that will position you to have global impact.

A *"Miracle Worker"* is a person who agrees to:
1. Financially support the ministry of New Wine International (NWI)
2. Pray faithfully for Joshua & Janet Angela Mills and the NWI Ministry Team as they carry the message of Jesus Christ around the world.
3. Pray for those who will receive ministry through NWI ministry events and resources.

Partnership is not only what you can do to help me, but also what I can do to help you. Becoming a *Miracle Worker* with NWI provides a covenant agreement between you and me. By being a *Miracle Worker,* you will connect with the anointing and glory on this ministry as I send you monthly updates and revelatory teachings on the glory realm. You will receive my continued prayer for you and your family and you will be linked with the unique anointing that is on this ministry for unusual signs and wonders.

There are currently several ways to partner with NWI. I want you to decide the partnership level according to what the Lord has placed in your heart to do.

In His Great Love,

Joshua Mills

P.S. *Call my office today to become a partner or register online so that I can send you a special **Miracle Worker** Welcome Package filled with special benefits and information.*

Toll-Free: **1-866-60-NEW-WINE**
Online 24/7:
www.NewWineInternational.org
www.PartnersInPraise.com

BOOKS BY JOSHUA MILLS

31 Days Of Health, Wealth & Happiness

31 Days To A Breakthrough Prayer Life

31 Days To A Miracle Mindset

Advanced School Of Miracles

Atmosphere

Into His Presence – Praise & Worship Manual

Ministry Resources 101

Personal Ministry Prayer Manual

Positioned For Prosperity

School Of Miracles, Volume I

School Of Miracles, Volume II

School Of Miracles, Volume III

School Of Signs & Wonders, Course I

School Of Signs & Wonders, Course II

Simple Supernatural

Simple Supernatural Study Guide

Third Day Prayers

Time & Eternity

Available online 24/7 at:

www.NewWineInternational.org

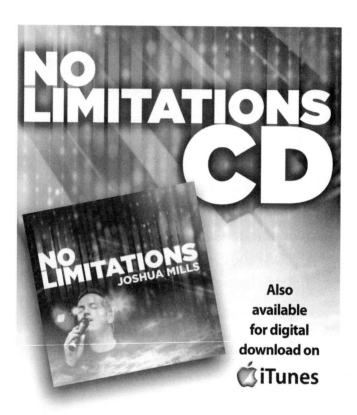

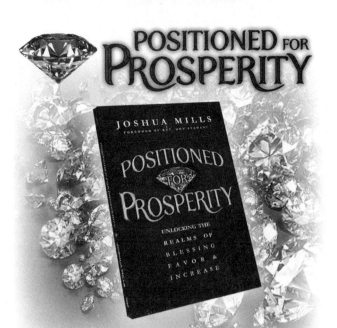

POSITIONED FOR PROSPERITY

JOSHUA MILLS
FOREWORD BY REV. DON STEWART

POSITIONED FOR PROSPERITY

UNLOCKING THE REALMS OF BLESSING FAVOR & INCREASE

Praise for these Best-selling Books...

"Joshua has identified simple, yet profound keys found in the Word of God that will help the reader receive an impartation to unlock the realms of success and happiness..."

- *Drs. Christian & Robin Harfouche (Senior Pastors, Miracle Faith Center, Pensacola, FL)*

"...31 Days Of Health, Wealth and Happiness is a helpful resource to assist you in your daily walk of faith... we recommend this book to you!"

- *Dr. Stephen & Kellie Swisher (Senior Executives, Kenneth Copeland Ministries)*

"The vibrant truths in this "breakthrough book" will undoubtedly create a desire to walk in the Word and the Spirit with a fresh and different perspective! Joshua Mills has gleaned them by experience, not simply as theories, and has the ability to impart them to us."

- *Mary Audrey Raycroft (Teaching Pastor, Catch The Fire Church, Toronto, ON)*

This is your personal reference guide for Holy Spirit led prayers and ministry to your every need!

- Understand how to pray effectively with confidence
- Have a world-changing prayer life and ministry!
- Tips for Intercessory Prayer Warriors
- Excellent resource for Bible Studies, Cell Groups and personal devotion
- Learn about the Glory Realm!

Call Toll-Free To Order Today!
1-866-60-NEW-WINE
www.NewWineInternational.org

THE PROPHETIC SOUND OF CHANGE...
SHIFTING THE ATMOSPHERE

Through Praise!

Filmed and recorded live from Paramount Pictures Studios in Hollywood, California.

Holy
Invasion -
Music CD

**Available on
CD and DVD**

One Night of
Heaven Invading
Hollywood - DVD

**Experience this
extraordinary sound of
praise in Hollywood**

as hosts Joshua and Janet Angela Mills usher
in the glory through spontaneous prophetic
worship, expressive dance and multi-sensory
media along with special guests: Steve
Swanson, Julie Meyer, JoAnn McFatter, LaRue
Howard, Georgian Banov, Alberto & Kimberly
Rivera and Davene Garland.

Includes the songs: Eye To Eye / Like A
Flood / Greater Glory / Step Into Me /
Rend The Veil / Alabaster Box / Hollywood
Prophecy / Paint Your Picture / In Your
Glory Realm / plus more...

www.NewWineInternational.org

Become a *Supernatural Mother* with...

Childbirth in the *Glory*

Janet Angela Mills

A Special "Supernatural Mother Package" is also available with additional resources.

This supernaturally anointed CD and book by Janet Angela Mills is full of God's promises for conception, pregnancy, delivery and dedication! For many women pregnancy is oftentimes a season of morning sickness, mood swings and stress followed by tremendous pain and hard labor. Some married couples have even been told that they can never conceive a child, while others have suffered the pain of one miscarriage after another. As a child of God this is not the way God intended for it to be! These resources contain promise scriptures and glory-filled declarations intended for a pain-free and supernatural Childbirth In The Glory!

These resources make great gifts for baby showers, dedications and those desiring to have children!

Order Online 24/7 at www.NewWineInternational.org

there is no spa like a...

SpiritSpa
rest | ease | rejuvenation

SpiritSpa ▶   ◀ SpiritSpa II

"...times of refreshing shall come from the presence of the Lord."
– Acts 3:19

"...I fully recommend SpiritSpa for every
massage therapist as well as anyone
else who is looking for music to aid in
relaxation."
Melody Barker, NCTM, LMT TX, LMT TN
Nationally Certified Massage Therapist,
Nashville, Tennessee

"...this music does in fact belong in
every spa across the country."
Shaun H.,
Radio Indy Music Review,
Encinitas, California

These CDs gently envelop and embrace you in a blanket of restful
peace. Linger in heavenly realms and indulge your spirit with these
soothing instrumental piano melodies. This beautiful music by
Joshua Mills is sure to calm the spirit, soul and body with God's
supernatural rest, ease and rejuvenation.

Call Toll-Free To Order Today! 1-866-60-NEW-WINE
www.NewWineInternational.org

Contact Information

To order more copies of
31 Days To A Miracle Mindset,
please visit the online store at:
www.IntensifiedGlory.com
or call toll-free:
1-866-60-NEW-WINE
(1-866-606-3994)

We have excellent bulk / wholesale discount-
ed prices for bookstores and ministries.
Please contact office@intensifiedglory.com
for more information.